THE *Carluccio's* COLLECTION

PASTA

ANTONIO & PRISCILLA CARLUCCIO

Dedicated to the memory of
photographer André Martin

Quadrille
PUBLISHING

Contents

All recipes are for 4 unless otherwise stated. Use either all metric or all imperial measures, as the two are not necessarily interchangeable.

Foreword

It is often claimed that Marco Polo brought pasta back to Italy from China. Nothing could be farther from the truth – in fact, it was already known to the Romans and the Greeks long before Marco Polo and his adventures. Then, however, without the now ubiquitous tomato, the ancient Romans enjoyed their pasta dressed with sauces based mainly on anchovies and garlic. Over time, pasta has become one of our staple foods, on a par with bread.

In ancient times pasta was hand-produced in Sicily in the shape of what we now call macaroni. However, the true birthplace of *pasta lunga*, like spaghetti and tagliatelle, has to be the region of Campania and more specifically the province of Napoli. The main ingredient of pasta, durum wheat grain, was growing abundantly in the region of Puglia and, since Naples had suitable sources of water and atmospheric conditions well suited to the drying process, pasta manufacturing flourished there.

On the northern Italian coast in Liguria, in contrast, pasta production developed as a result of imports. Thanks to its mighty and powerful merchant navy, Liguria was able to import Russian and Turkish grains equally suited to pasta-making. It was in these two regions that the pasta tradition started to be industrialized to satisfy the ever-growing demand.

When tomatoes were eventually brought to Italy from the New World, they became inextricably linked with pasta and their horticulture flourished. At the time of the unification of Italy as a Republic in 1861 under Garibaldi, pasta with tomatoes became the national dish and was to be found in every region.

The durum wheat semolina from which most pasta is made is a grain with a particular gluten content; it is nutritionally balanced and maintains its shape and structure after cooking. The cooking time for pasta is normally adjusted to allow it to remain *al dente*, indicating that the pasta is cooked but still offers a certain resistance to the bite.

Almost everyone enjoys a good plate of pasta with a delicious sauce and it is also good for you; athletes often make good use of pasta as part of their diet, since its complex carbohydrates provide nourishment and energy in a form that is slowly digested and absorbed by the body, enhancing and maintaining energy levels for competition and training.

There are about 600 different shapes of pasta in Italy, and each is suited to a different type of sauce. For example, pasta shapes such as penne or rigatoni are best with thicker, heavier sauces that stick to the short shapes and also get caught inside the tubes. Spaghetti and tagliatelle are better with more 'slithery' sauces. Try to think about the consistency of your sauce and use a shape of pasta that is well suited to it. You will find that certain pastas and sauces 'marry' together well – see the guide to matching pasta sauces to types of pasta on page 13.

The way pasta is used also differs between the regions: besides the classic dishes – like *spaghetti alla carbonara*, or with *pesto* or with tomatoes and basil (my favourite!), there are literally thousands of recipes combining meat, fish, game, cheese or vegetables, and these are often shaped by the region's local produce.

Italians eat about 30 kilos of pasta per person per year. Considering that you need about 100 grams of dry pasta for a normal first-course portion, this means that Italians must eat pasta at least 300 days of the year! In Britain, however, the amount consumed is a tenth of that. I do hope that this book will inspire you to raise the level of pasta consumption in this country!

One day recently, the BBC World Service telephoned to ask me about 'World Pasta Day'. Although I am aware that pasta is becoming a global food, I didn't know until then that such a day existed. Judging by the way in which pasta has conquered the world, it looks like its development over the last two centuries in Italy has finally converted the taste-buds of billions of people – rich and poor alike.

In this book you will find a wealth of suggestions to help you create a perfect plate of pasta, just as the Italians like it – discover your own favourite combination! Once you have mastered pasta with sauces, why not try your hand at making your own pasta, either plain or stuffed – it's great fun and you will be amply rewarded when you sit down to a mouth-watering plate of home-made pasta!

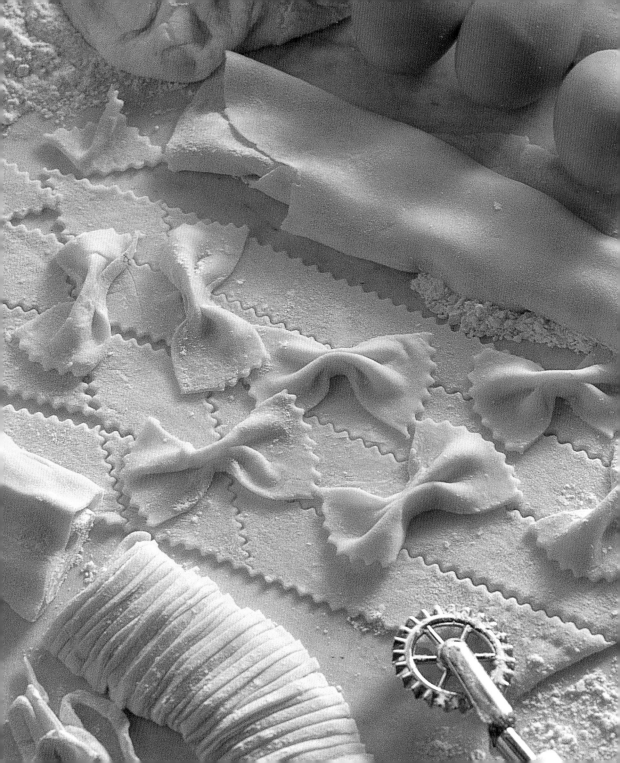

How to Make Fresh Egg Pasta

300 g (10½ oz) 00 (doppio zero) flour, plus more for dusting
3 eggs
pinch of salt

Sift the flour on to a work surface (marble is ideal), forming it into a volcano-shaped mound with a well in the centre. Break the eggs into this well and add the salt.

With your hands, incorporate the eggs into the flour, gradually drawing the flour into the egg until it forms a coarse paste. Add a little more flour if the mixture seems too soft or sticky. With a spatula, scrape together all the dough.

Clean your hands and the work surface. Lightly dust the work surface with flour again and then knead the dough with the heels of your hands, giving it lots of shoulder power. Work the dough for 10–15 minutes, until the consistency is smooth and elastic. Wrap the dough in cling film or foil and leave it to rest for about 30 minutes.

Lightly flour the work surface again and a rolling pin. Gently roll out the rested dough, rotating it by quarter turns, to obtain a round sheet of pasta with a thickness of 2 or 3 mm. Cut the sheets into noodles, or use to make lasagne, ravioli, etc., as described in the other recipes that follow.

Makes about 500 g (1 lb)

Lucia wrapping freshly made ravioli for a customer at the Pastificio Defilippis, Turin's celebrated specialist pasta shop.

The finest fresh egg pasta is made at home, using the best and freshest of ingredients.

How To Cook Pasta

Pasta has to be cooked in plenty of rapidly boiling salted water — allow 1 litre (1¾ pints) of water and 1 tablespoon of salt for every 100 g (3½ oz) of pasta. Add the salt just before the pasta. It is also important that the pan is large enough for the water to remain at a good rolling boil to ensure the pasta moves around as it cooks. As pasta exudes starch as it cooks, the amount of water used in relation to the pasta is significant. If there is too little water in the pan, it becomes clogged by the starch and the pasta does not cook properly.

Let the pasta fall gently into the water rather than feeding in clumps which will encourage it to stick together. Gently curl long strands down into the water. Put the lid on to get the water back to the boil as quickly as possible. As soon as it is boiling again, remove the lid and loosen the pasta with a fork. Never add oil to the water, unless cooking large sheets of lasagne which may stick together.

Timing is all-important in cooking pasta. Fresh egg pasta cooks in a couple of minutes, or even less if it is very fine. When using fresh egg pasta, make sure the sauce is ready before you cook the pasta and that your guests are at the table. Pasta is cooked when it is *al dente*, that is tender but offering a little resistance to the bite.

When the pasta is cooked, take off the heat and add a cup of cold water to stop the cooking, then wait for half a minute before draining. Don't rinse the pasta or you will strip it of flavour and nutrients. Reserve the cooking water to adjust the texture of the sauce (just drained pasta continues to absorb moisture, so a sauce which was the right consistency before being added to the pasta can suddenly seem too thick).

The range of pasta on sale at Pastificio Defilippis is bewildering to the newcomer.

Types of Pasta

Pasta di semola di grano duro secca *(dried durum wheat semolina pasta)*
This is the basic dried pasta made from a flour-and-water mixture, using durum wheat semolina. *Pasta lunga* (long pasta) like spaghetti and tagliatelle should still be flexible when bent and should have a glowing amber colour.

Pasta di semola fresca *(fresh durum wheat pasta)*
This is made from a dough of fresh semolina and water, and is usually handmade in the south of Italy.

Pasta all'uovo secca *(dried egg pasta)*
The combination of durum wheat semolina and eggs is only produced commercially, as the very firm dough needs to be worked by machine.

Pasta fresca all'uovo *(fresh egg pasta)*
Fresh egg pasta is made using eggs and 00 *(doppio zero)* flour, the same tender wheat used to make cakes, rather than durum semolina.

Matching sauces to pasta types

Thin egg ribbons, like tagliolini, are mostly served with truffles, butter and parmesan, or light fresh tomato sauces.

Thicker ribbons, like tagliatelle, are good with sauces of tomato, mushroom, cheese, cream, ham and fish, and with Bolognese.

Long flat dried pasta, like trenette or linguine, really suit pesto.

Long pastas like spaghetti, are best with tomato-based ragùs.

Tubes, like rigatoni, are made for long-cooked ragùs of tomato, etc.

Short shapes of pure semolina pasta, like cavatelli and orecchiette, are very good with vegetable and seafood sauces.

Stuffed pastas, like ravioli, need only simple sauces like the juices from a roast or butter and sage, or a light tomato sauce.

Eating Pasta

When eating long pasta, as soon as it arrives in front of you, loosen it on the plate to distribute the sauce evenly. Then, lift a few strands and push them to the side of your plate to make some space to turn the fork. Twist the pasta strands around the fork and put the curled ball of pasta elegantly into your mouth. Never allow strands to hang from your mouth nor cut long strands with your teeth. The use of a spoon with the fork is considered impolite by Italians.

Pasta e Fagioli

PASTA AND BEAN SOUP

200 g (7 oz) dried cannellini beans or 400 g (14 oz) fresh beans
90 ml (3 fl oz) extra-virgin olive oil
2 garlic cloves, finely chopped
1 small chilli, finely chopped
2 celery stalks with leaves, finely chopped
1 carrot, finely chopped
2 large tomatoes, peeled, deseeded and chopped, or 1 tbsp tomato paste
2 basil leaves, plus extra to decorate
300 g (10½ oz) mixed pasta
salt and pepper

Soak the beans in water to cover for 12 hours if using dried. Then drain, cover with fresh water and cook for about 2 hours or until tender. If using fresh, simmer for 30–40 minutes until cooked. Purée about a quarter of the cooked beans in a liquidizer, then set aside.

Heat the oil in a pan, add the garlic, chilli, celery, carrot and tomato and fry for a few minutes. Add 1 litre (1¾ pints) water with seasoning to taste, then stir in the whole and puréed beans with the basil. Bring to the boil, add the pasta and simmer for 8–10 minutes, until *al dente*. Let rest briefly, then sprinkle with basil to serve.

When I arranged the wedding meal for my stepson and his wife. I added pasta shapes of their initials and some love hearts to the soup.

Pasta for Soup

This recipe, the Neapolitan version of this classic dish, is a good way of using up odds and ends of different pasta shapes, known as munnezzaglia *in the Neapolitan dialect.*

Perhaps the best-known use of pasta in soup is pastina in brodo. *The* brodo *(broth) can be of chicken, veal, beef, or other meats. In this stock are cooked any of the following types of pasta, specifically designed to cook in a short time:* anellini *(little rings),* avemarie *and* tubettini *(short tubes),* conchigliette *(small shells),* cuoricini *(tiny hearts),* diavolini *(little devils),* farfalline *(baby butterflies),* grandine *(hailstones),* lumachine *(small snails),* pepe *(peppercorns),* pepe bucato *(peppercorns with a hole),* perline *(pearls),* puntine *(points),* quadrettini *(squares),* stelline *(stars), as well as* seme d'avena *(oat grains),* d'orzo *(barley),* di riso *(rice),* di mele *(apple seed),* di melone *(melon seeds) and* di peperone *(pepper seeds) and many, many others.*

Alfabeto, small pasta in the shapes of letters of the alphabet, is also popular in soup, especially for children.

Vegetable Pasta Sauces

Arrabbiata

Heat 3 tablespoons of olive oil in a pan, add 1 small onion, thinly sliced, fresh or dried chilli to taste and 1 garlic clove, coarsely chopped, and fry for 1 minute. Stir in 600 g (1¼ lb) tomatoes, skinned, deseeded and finely chopped and cook for 6–8 minutes, then add 6 basil leaves, coarsely chopped, and some salt. Penne is the classic pasta to dress with this 'angry' sauce. No Parmesan here!

Puttanesca

This typically Roman sauce gets its name from the Italian for a whore. Make as Arrabbiata above, but replacing the basil with 20 chopped black olives and 10 large salted capers, chopped. It goes very well with spaghetti *al dente*.

Napoletana

Heat 3 tablespoons of olive oil in a pan and gently fry 2 crushed garlic cloves for a few minutes without allowing them to colour. Add 1 kg (2¼ lb) tomatoes, skinned, deseeded and chopped and fry, stirring constantly, for 5 minutes, allowing just the excess liquid to evaporate. Add 6 basil leaves and salt and pepper to taste and the sauce is ready for use for the most wonderful plate of spaghetti or many other dishes. The Neapolitans, however, use their *ragù* mostly on large pasta shapes like rigatoni, candele and ziti.

Chilli Pepper

It is thought that chilli was brought back from America by Christopher Columbus. It quickly became known as la droga dei poveri, *'the poor man's drug', because of its powerful taste that could flavour any food, however dull. It also had the extra benefit of stimulating digestion as well as acting as a disinfectant. In Italy, the further south you go, the more this powerful 'drug' is used. There it is used as a condiment and offered on the tables of restaurants along with the salt and pepper. The peppers can often be seen hanging in long strings from people's balconies and windows.*

19

Orecchiette con Broccoli

ORECCHIETTE WITH BROCCOLI

500 g (1 lb) broccoli florets
90 ml (3 fl oz) extra-virgin olive oil
2 garlic cloves, finely chopped
1 small chilli, finely chopped or sliced
500 g (1 lb) orecchiette, or other Apulian cavatelli pasta
salt
freshly grated pecorino cheese (optional)

Cook the broccoli in lightly salted boiling water until tender, then drain. Put the oil in a pan over a low heat, then add the garlic and chilli and cook gently for a few minutes until softened. Add the broccoli florets and mix well. Season with salt to taste.

Cook the pasta in boiling salted water for 14–18 minutes, until *al dente*, then drain, mix with the broccoli sauce and serve, with grated pecorino cheese if desired.

Cavatelli

This typical Southern pasta shape is now also popular in the North because it is ideal for serving with vegetable sauces like those made with broccoli, rocket, courgette and aubergine. In the southern regions of Puglia and Sicily, cavatelli like orecchiette is served with a rich tomato sauce made with the very best local ingredients. It also goes well with seafood, especially mussels.

In Puglia, broccoli and orecchiette are almost synonymous. The combination of pasta and the very strong flavours of local broccoli, tomatoes, olive oil and some chilli makes it a really wonderful dish.

Pine Nut

The pine nut or kernel is the seed of the pine tree. It is held in the familiar pine cone, made up of a series of wooden tongues. The creamy-white kernel is about 1 cm (½ inch) long and slightly pointed at one end. The seed can only be gathered from the cones of mature trees at least 70 years of age, which is why the nut is not cultivated on a large scale. The trees are part of the Ombrella family and are typical of the landscape of the coastal regions of Tuscany, Campania and Sicily. The kernel can only be harvested if the cone is completely open when it is collected, although a short spell in a hot oven will encourage it to open to release the seeds.

Despite its high fat content, the pine nut is very nutritious, having a high proportion of proteins, vitamins and minerals. Always make sure you buy fresh pine nuts as their fat can turn rancid, making them inedible. The pine nut has been popular as an ingredient since biblical times and is often used along with raisins as a flavouring for meat, and to make stuffings for meat and poultry. This is a reminder of Arab influences on Southern Italian cooking. In Liguria, pine nuts are an essential ingredient for the famous pesto sauce (see opposite).

Pesto alla Genovese con Trofie

PESTO WITH TROFIE PASTA

400 g (14 oz) trofie pasta

FOR THE PESTO:

45 g (1½ oz) freshly picked basil leaves, preferably Ligurian small-leaved basil

10 g (⅓ oz) coarse sea salt

25 g (¾ oz) pine nuts, toasted

2 garlic cloves, roughly chopped

55 g (1¾ oz) parmesan cheese, grated (if you prefer a stronger sauce, use pecorino instead)

125 ml (4 fl oz) Ligurian extra-virgin olive oil

You could put all the ingredients for the pesto in a food processor and after a few seconds it is all over. However, the taste of real pesto is obtained using a pestle and mortar. Put the dry basil leaves in a mortar with the salt, pine nuts and garlic. Rotate the pestle to grind all the ingredients, using the salt at the bottom of the mortar to help break them down. Work like this for a while until you see a pulp starting to form. Still working with the pestle, add the cheese a little at a time and pound until it has all been absorbed and a thick paste has formed. Now start to pour in the oil a little at a time and work with the pestle until it has all been absorbed.

Cook the pasta in boiling salted water until *al dente*, then drain, keeping 2 or 3 tablespoons of the cooking water. Put the pesto in a pan, dilute with the reserved cooking water and just warm through. Mix with the pasta and serve.

Trofie Pasta

Handmade using a dough of 00 (doppio zero) flour and water, sometimes with the addition of potato purée, trofie are little pieces of dough twisted to look like tiny spirals with pointed ends. To make these Ligurian specialities, roll some fresh dough in the palm of your hand until it is long and thin, like spaghetti. Cut it into 4-cm (1½-inch) chunks and roll them again with your fingers to make the spiral shape and the pointed ends. They are eaten mostly with pesto sauce but are also very good with other sauces, called tocchi *in Liguria, including* tocco di noce, *a walnut sauce, also used to savour* pansôti al preboggion *(see pages 36–7).*

Penne con Pinoli e Melanzane

PENNE WITH PINE NUTS AND AUBERGINE

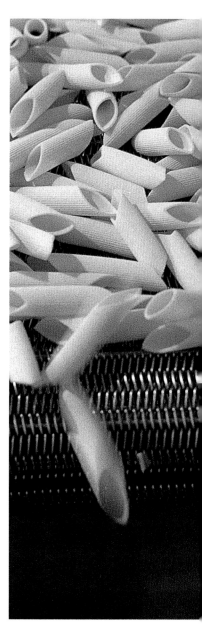

400 g (14 oz) aubergine, cut into small cubes

90 ml (3 fl oz) extra-virgin olive oil

1 garlic clove, finely chopped

3 tbsp tomato paste

25 g (¾ oz) pine nuts

10 large salted capers, soaked in water for 10 minutes, then drained
and chopped

1 small chilli, finely chopped

20 black olives, stoned

400 g (14 oz) penne

60 g (2 oz) mature pecorino cheese, freshly grated

Leave the aubergine cubes in lightly salted water for 1 hour, then
drain, squeeze out the water and pat dry on paper towels. Fry them
in the oil with the garlic until brown. Add the tomato paste, pine
nuts, capers, chilli and olives and fry gently for 10 minutes. Add a
little water if the mixture is too dry.

Cook the pasta in boiling salted water until *al dente*, then drain
and mix well with the sauce. Serve with the grated cheese.

After spaghetti, penne is arguably the next
best-known pasta shape in the world.

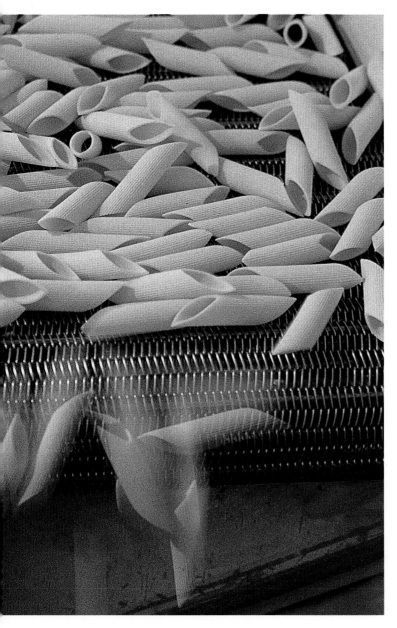

Penne

Penne are tubes of pasta cut at an angle so that they have pointed ends, like a quill. It comes in two varieties, penne lisce (smooth) and penne rigate (ribbed) and in many different sizes. The smallest are pennettine and pennine and the largest penne di ziti, penne a candela and penne di natale – which has a huge length of 15–18 cm (6–7 inches).

Penne are most popular in Liguria and Campania, where there are many recipes for sauces, including the Campanian sauces based on tomatoes with meat and chilli. The smaller varieties, called pennette, are best served in a much lighter fresh tomato sauce with basil and little cubes of mozzarella which melt when they come into contact with the hot pasta. Penne are also used for timbales.

Another dish, penne all'arrabbiata ('angry penne'), is penne with a very hot chilli sauce (see page 18), the anger in the name suggesting the ferocity of the heat, which can, of course, be adapted according to taste. It is perhaps due to the popularity of penne all'arrabbiata in both Italy and now abroad, that penne have become so popular throughout the world.

This dish is one of the ways in which Sicilians honour the sardine.

Pasta con le Sarde
PASTA WITH SARDINES

12 fresh sardines, tops and tails removed, gutted and boned

100 g (3½ oz) wild fennel leaves, plus more to garnish

1 onion, finely chopped

2 tbsp currants

2 tbsp pine nuts

6 anchovy fillets, chopped

150 g (5 oz) tomato paste, dissolved in a cup of lukewarm water

1 tsp freshly grated nutmeg

500 g (1 lb) maccheroncini or bucatini

salt and pepper

flour for coating

olive oil for frying

Fennel

As well as using the bulb of one variety as a vegetable, both the leaves and seeds of the fennel plant are widely used in Italy, where it can be found growing wild in the South beside country roads. Its flavour is less sweet than that of the very similar aniseed, to which it is related. The seeds are longer and a distinctive pale green when dried.

Fennel is popular in the cooking of Tuscany and the South, to flavour pork dishes and the famous Tuscan salami called finocchiona, as well as other fresh and preserved sausages. In Puglia and the South it is much used to make taralli, *the local savoury biscuits, as well as bread and sweet biscuits.*

Open the sardines out flat. Coat them lightly in flour. Heat a good amount of olive oil in a large frying pan and fry the sardines until golden brown on each side. Drain on paper towels and keep warm.

Cook the fennel in boiling water for about 20 minutes or until soft, then drain, reserving the cooking water. Finely chop the fennel.

Heat 2 tablespoons of oil in a large pan, add the onion and fry gently until soft. Stir in the fennel, currants, pine nuts, anchovies, tomato paste mixture and a little of the fennel water. Break up 6 of the sardines into the pan. Mix well to make a fairly thick sauce and heat through. If too thick, add a little more of the fennel water. Season with the nutmeg and a little salt and some pepper.

Cook the pasta in boiling salted water until *al dente*, then drain and mix into the sauce. Serve decorated with the remaining sardines. Serves 6

Strangozzi all'Acciuga e Peperone

STRANGOZZI WITH ANCHOVY AND PEPPERS

Bigoli

This popular pasta, originally from Mantova in Emilia-Romagna, is a whole-wheat egg pasta that looks like a large, fat spaghetti. In the past, the pasta dough would have been handmade and forced through a little machine called a torchio *or* bigolaro, *but today it is also produced commercially. Among many specialities from the region using bigoli there is the Venetian dish* bigoli in salsa, *in which it is served with a sauce of onions, olive oil and anchovies.*

Similarly shaped handmade pastas include the variously named pinci, ciriole, cirioline and strangozzi, stringozzi or strengozzi, as they are called in Umbria and Tuscany. These are quite large, with a diameter of about 4 mm (⅛ inch). Unlike bigoli, they are made from a dough of durum wheat, water and a little olive oil, and are long and have an irregular shape, obtained by rolling and stretching the dough. In Umbria, strengozzi are served with Norcia truffle, or ragùs of wild boar, rabbit, mushroom and, naturally, tomato.

2 tbsp extra-virgin olive oil
1 garlic clove, finely chopped
1 small chilli, finely chopped
3 red peppers, roasted, skinned and sliced
8 anchovy fillets, finely chopped
500 g (1 lb) strangozzi or similar hard durum wheat pasta such as pinci or bigoli
1 tbsp coarsely chopped flat-leaf parsley

Heat the olive oil in a pan, add the garlic, chilli and roasted peppers and fry gently until they are turning slightly brown. Add the anchovies and let them dissolve over a gentle heat.

Cook the pasta in boiling salted water until *al dente*, then drain, reserving a couple of tablespoons of the cooking water to dilute the sauce. Add the pasta and reserved cooking liquid to the sauce and toss well, then mix in the parsley and serve. You may add salt if you wish, but be careful because the anchovies are salty.

Great care has to be taken when cooking strangozzi as, being made without eggs, they break up readily.

Linguine con Aragosta
LINGUINE WITH LOBSTER

1 live lobster, weighing about 1.25 kg (2½ lb), or 2 lobsters
    weighing 600 g (1¼ lb) each
½ garlic clove, finely chopped
90 ml (3 fl oz) extra-virgin olive oil
1 glass of white wine
700 g (1½ lb) tomatoes, skinned, deseeded and chopped
400 g (14 oz) linguine or bavette
1 tbsp coarsely chopped flat-leaf parsley
salt and pepper

Bavette

*Bavette, linguine or lingue di passero
(sparrows' tongues) is a long pasta like a
thick flattened spaghetti, with an oval section rather than round, giving a lovely
mellow sensation to the palate. Its shape
makes it particularly good with pesto and
seafood sauces. Smaller sizes are called
bavettine, linguettine and linguette, while
a Genovese version is called trenette and is
almost exclusively eaten with pesto.*

Bring a large pan of lightly salted water to the boil. Put the lobster in, cover and simmer for 15–25 minutes, depending on size. Remove the lobster (reserving the water) and leave to cool, then cut it in half lengthwise and remove the 2 gills (near the head), the dark vein running down the tail and the small stomach sac in the head. Do not discard the green, creamy liver in the head. Take out the tail meat, then crack open the claws and remove the meat. Cut it into small chunks.

Briefly fry the garlic in the oil without browning. Add the wine and bubble for a minute. Stir in the tomatoes and simmer for 10 minutes. Add the lobster meat, liver and shells, and heat through gently. Season.

Cook the pasta in the lobster water. Discard the shells from the sauce, season and mix with the drained pasta. Serve sprinkled with parsley.

You will find versions of this classic pasta dish in most coastal regions, cooked in many different ways. This is the simplest.

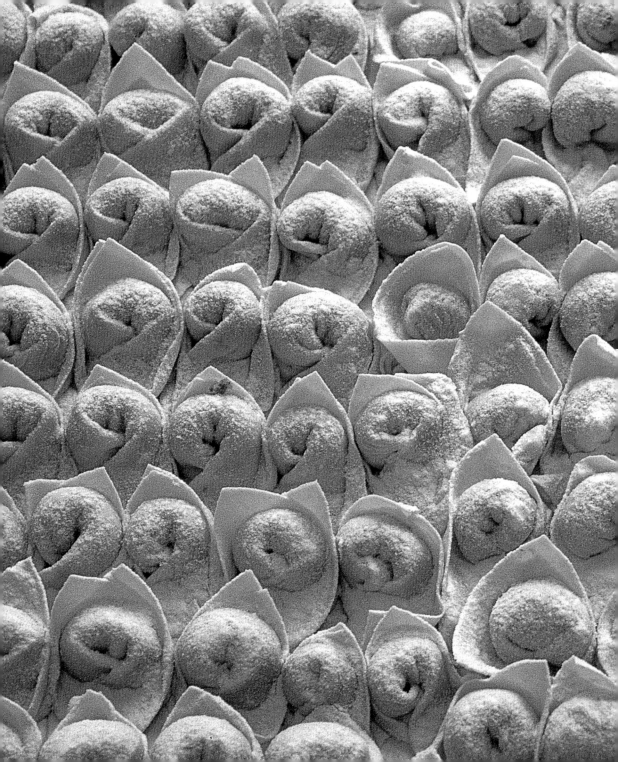

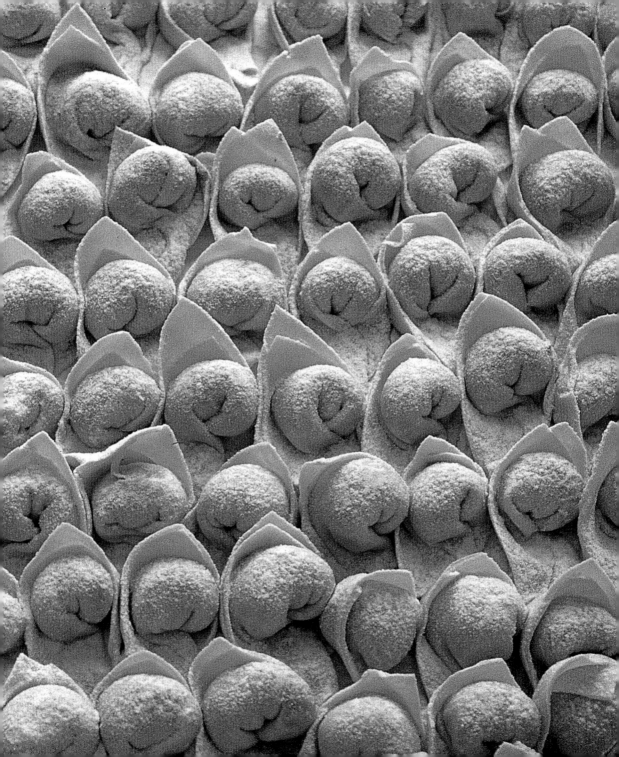

Pansôti al Preboggion

PASTA STUFFED WITH MIXED GREENS

Pansôti

This stuffed pasta, typical of Liguria, may either take the form of a triangle or be shaped like tortellini. Their name actually comes from pansa, *a Ligurian dialect word meaning 'tummy', from their shape. The classic stuffing is* preboggion, *a mixture of wild local greens including borage, with parmesan. This is traditionally served with* tocco di noce, *a walnut sauce.*

1 kg (2¼ lb) mixed greens (see right)

250 g (9 oz) ricotta cheese

60 g (2 oz) parmesan cheese, grated

2 eggs

1 recipe quantity of basic pasta dough (see page 9)

FOR THE SAUCE:

175 g (6 oz) walnuts, blanched and peeled

70 g (2½ oz) pine nuts

breadcrumbs from 1 fresh bread roll

1 very small garlic clove, finely chopped

a few marjoram or thyme leaves

4 tbsp strained Greek yoghurt

extra-virgin olive oil, to dilute

salt and pepper

First make the sauce: blend together the walnuts, pine nuts, bread-crumbs, garlic and herbs using a pestle and mortar until they are reduced to a thick paste. Gradually work in the yoghurt and then enough oil to give a smooth, fairly thick sauce. Season to taste.

For the pansôti, cook the greens in boiling water until tender, drain and squeeze out excess water. Chop very finely and combine with the ricotta, parmesan, eggs and some seasoning. Mix to a fairly stiff paste.

Roll the pasta into long sheets about 2 mm (1½ inch) thick. Cut out circles 7.5 cm (3 inches) in diameter, divide the filling between them, then fold in half to make half-moons, pressing the edges well to seal.

Gently warm the sauce. Cook the pansôti in boiling salted water for 5–6 minutes, until *al dente*, drain and mix with the sauce. Serve immediately.

These small, tummy-shaped ravioli are filled with a typical
Ligurian mixture of wild herbs and vegetables such as fresh borage,
Swiss chard and dandelion. You could use spinach and other greens.

Pumpkin

Pumpkin is popular in Piedmont, where the whole thing is baked in the oven and the cooked flesh spooned out, in the Veneto where they serve it with pickles, and in Lombardy, where they use it to make risotto. In Campania it is called cocozza, *and is sliced and lightly boiled then fried. It is also known as* salmone di campagna *or country salmon, because of its orange-red colour. In Emilia-Romagna it is used to make* tortelli di zucca *(see overleaf), which uses cooked pumpkin mixed with* mostarda.

A dish of Raviolo Aperto con Funghi (pages 42–3) surrounded by Tortelli di Zucca and Agnolotti Piemontesi al Burro e Salvia (overleaf).

Tortelli di Zucca

PUMPKIN RAVIOLI

Tortelli

The diversity of this type of pasta ranges from tordello, a Tuscan half-moon raviolo made from an egg pasta and filled with a mixture of Swiss chard or spinach, ricotta, pecorino, veal, brains and spices, to tortelli di magro (meaning lean, without meat) which are usually filled with ricotta, spinach, eggs and cheese. Tortellini is a smaller version of the same pasta, while tortelloni are the largest. The sweet tortelli di San Giuseppe, filled with ricotta, sugar and spices, are fried in oil.

Cappellacci are a handmade round or triangular version of this type of pasta, originally from Emilia-Romagna. The filling used is generally similar to the one used here, Cappellacci are served with melted butter, sage and more parmesan.

1.75 kg (4 lb) pumpkin, cut into large slices
6 amaretti biscuits, finely crumbled
100 g (3½ oz) parmesan cheese, grated
55 g (1¾ oz) mostarda di Cremona (mustard fruits), finely diced
60 g (2 oz) butter
12 sage leaves
FOR THE PASTA DOUGH:
600 g (1¼ lb) 00 (doppio zero) flour
4 eggs

Preheat the oven to 200°C/400°F/gas 6. Bake the pumpkin for about 40 minutes, until soft. Scrape the flesh off the rind, put it in a colander and squeeze out most of the moisture. Mix with the amaretti, half the parmesan and the mostarda to make a compact paste.

Make the pasta as on page 9, adding enough water to make a soft dough. Roll out into very thin sheets and cut out discs about 6 cm (2½ inches) in diameter. Place a little filling to one side of each, then fold in half, pinching the edges together to seal.

Cook the tortelli in plenty of boiling salted water for 6–7 minutes, until *al dente*, then drain. Put the butter and sage in a large pan and heat until the butter is foaming. Add the tortelli and mix to coat. Transfer to serving plates and sprinkle with the remaining cheese.

The pasta dough here is softer than the basic dough, making it particularly suitable for these delicate ravioli.

Agnolotti Piemontesi al Burro e Salvia

PIEDMONTESE RAVIOLI WITH BUTTER AND SAGE

300 g (10½ oz) spinach or swiss chard leaves

300 g (10½ oz) left-over cooked beef

85 g (3 oz) cooked chicken breast

100 g (3½ oz) cooked sausage, or fresh sausage, such as luganiga

2 eggs

85 g (3 oz) parmesan cheese, grated

1 recipe quantity of basic pasta dough (see page 9)

60 g (2 oz) butter

10 sage leaves

salt and pepper

freshly grated nutmeg

Agnolotti

The original idea with this type of pasta was to use any leftovers of meat and sausage to make a very economical dish.

Agnolotti are usually eaten either with melted butter, sage and parmesan, with a light tomato sauce or even better with the deglazed juices from a roasted joint. Similar pastas include the Sardinian angiulottus and culingiones, the Tuscan tordelli, the Ligurian ravioli, and tortelli from Emilia-Romagna. Rather confusingly, a smaller version of agnolotti are called tortellini, while a larger type are called tortelloni.

Cook the spinach or chard leaves in boiling salted water until tender, drain and squeeze out excess liquid. Mince or very finely chop all the meat and the greens. Put in a bowl and stir in the eggs and 30 g (1 oz) of the parmesan, plus nutmeg, salt and pepper to taste. Set aside.

Dust a work surface with flour and roll out 2 long thin sheets of pasta. Place teaspoons of the filling at 2.5-cm (1-inch) intervals in rows along one sheet of pasta, then cover with the other sheet and press gently round each pile of filling, making sure the pasta sticks together all around it. Cut into squares with a serrated pastry wheel.

Cook the pasta in plenty of boiling salted water for 6–7 minutes, until *al dente*, then drain. Put the butter and sage leaves in a large pan and heat until the butter is foaming. Add the cooked agnolotti and mix to coat with the butter. Transfer to serving plates and sprinkle with the remaining grated parmesan cheese.

Serves 6

Raviolo Aperto con Funghi
OPEN RAVIOLO WITH MUSHROOMS

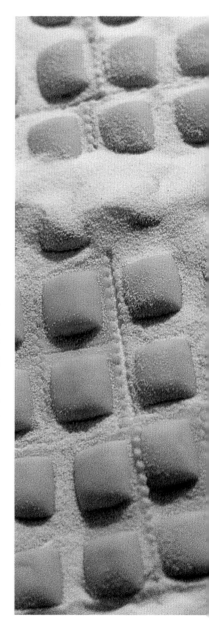

600 g (1¼ lb) mixed wild mushrooms, cleaned

60 g (2 oz) butter

1 garlic clove, finely chopped

1 tbsp tomato paste

1 tbsp chopped flat-leaf parsley

1 small glass of white wine

8 thin sheets of fresh pasta dough, 15 cm (6 inches) square (see page 9)

55 g (1¾ oz) parmesan cheese, grated (optional)

salt and pepper

Cut the mushrooms in half if large; otherwise leave them whole. Heat the butter in a pan, add the garlic and fry gently until softened but not browned. Add the mushrooms and stir-fry for 5 minutes, then add the tomato paste, parsley and some salt and pepper. Pour in the wine, bring to the boil and let it bubble for a few minutes.

Cook the sheets of pasta in boiling salted water until *al dente*, then drain. Carefully lay 4 sheets of pasta on 4 hot serving plates. Divide the mushroom mixture between them, reserving some of the sauce. Top the mushrooms with the remaining sheets of pasta and brush the top with the remaining sauce. Sprinkle with parmesan cheese if desired and serve immediately.

Ravioli

After spaghetti, ravioli are probably among the most successful of pastas worldwide. You can find genuine ravioli in almost every respectable restaurant and with every filling you could desire. Raviolini, one of the smallest of the square stuffed pastas, is usually eaten in brodo *(in broth) and ravioloni, the largest, are traditionally dressed with melted butter, sage and parmesan cheese. These little pasta parcels are called ravioli in most regions, with the exception of Piedmont where they are called agnolotti.*

My own version of raviolo is called raviolo aperto (open raviolo, see left). Two large squares of pasta the size of a plate are cooked in water, one is laid on the bottom of the plate, and the filling, which can be of meat, fish or mushrooms, cooked separately, placed in the centre and covered loosely with the other pasta square.

Meat Pasta Sauces

Carbonara

Like the amatriciana sauce below, *pasta alla carbonara* is another speciality of the Lazio region, making use of *guanciale*, air-dried pig cheek. About 100 g (4 oz) diced pork (nowadays usually replaced with pancetta) is cubed and fried in 2 tablespoons of oil until crisp. This is then stirred into a seasoned mixture of 3 beaten eggs and 85 g (3 oz) grated pecorino let down with a little of the pasta cooking water. The freshly drained pasta, traditionally bucatini, is then stirred into the sauce so that the egg mixture just coats the pasta but does not cook.

Ragù alla Bolognese

From the French *ragoût* or meat stew, this term has been adopted for long-cooked rich sauces, especially in Emilia-Romagna for their universally renowned *ragù alla Bolognese* and in Naples for their *ragù alla napoletana* (a sauce of tomatoes, meat, herbs and other flavourings, see page 18). *Ragù Bolognese*, made using minced veal or beef and pork, is mainly used to savour tagliatelle in the North. For a detailed recipe see page 55.

Amatriciana

Pasta alla amatriciana is a speciality of the Lazio region, particularly the town of Amatrice, after which it is named. Heat 3 tablespoons of oil and fry 150 g (5 oz) pancetta or bacon, cut in strips, with a chopped onion and chopped chilli for 3–4 minutes until slightly brown. Add 450 g (1 lb) pulped tomatoes and simmer gently for 10–15 minutes. It is traditionally served on bucatini and dressed with pecorino cheese.

Pecorino

This cheese is so popular that almost every region makes its own version, each adapted to suit local ingredients and culinary traditions. Wherever it comes from, pecorino is made in the same way. The difference in flavour between each one comes from the qualities in the local milks and the ageing processes. Pecorino is a compact white semi-cooked hard cheese made with full-fat milk. It is aged for at least 8 months before being eaten at table or grated like parmesan.

By law, pecorino romano can only be made in Lazio in the provinces of Rome, Frosinone, Grosseto, Latina and Viterbo. Exceptionally, romano-style pecorino is also made in Sardinia.

Sardinia's own pecorino is called fiore sardo or cacio fiore and is produced in the same way as other pecorinos, except that it is formed into much smaller rounds.

Ciriole al Ragù di Cinghiale

CIRIOLE PASTA WITH WILD BOAR SAUCE

3 tbsp virgin olive oil

1 onion, chopped

1 garlic clove, crushed

10 juniper berries

pinch of freshly grated nutmeg

pinch of ground cinnamon

4 fresh bay leaves, plus more to garnish

2 tbsp tomato paste

675 g (1½ lb) minced wild boar

250 ml (9 fl oz) red wine

150 ml (¼ pint) chicken stock

500 g (1 lb) ciriole pasta (see Bigoli, page 30)

salt and pepper

freshly grated pecorino cheese, to serve (optional)

Heat the oil in a large pan, add the onion, garlic, spices and bay leaves and fry gently until the onion is softened. Add the tomato paste, meat, wine and stock and simmer gently for about 1½ hours. Season to taste. Cook the pasta in boiling salted water until *al dente*, then drain. Add to the sauce, mix well and serve, sprinkled with some pecorino cheese if desired.

Almost every Tuscan and Umbrian family keeps frozen wild boar to make a *ragù*.

Wild Boar

Given that Italians love pork of any description, either cooked or preserved, it is not surprising that the wild version, wild boar, excites them so much. Sometimes considered pests, boar live in the hilly woods of Tuscany, Umbria, Abruzzo, and any other area where there is thick, inaccessible undergrowth in which they can hide and feed on juicy, tender shoots and berries.

Hunting wild boar can be dangerous because this animal, when under pressure, will attack humans. Boar-hunting is, however, a major sport in the regions of Sardinia, Sicily and Calabria, and a successful hunt is accompanied by enthusiastic celebrations.

In Tuscany, wild boar is used to produce many foods, including hams, salamis and salamini. While fresh it is wonderful in stews and ragùs, such as ciriole al ragù di cinghiale *(left) and to serve with the famous pinci pasta, handmade giant spaghetti. Due to large demand for wild boar, many half-wild boar are farmed in enclosed woody areas, leading a semi-wild life, producing a less gamy meat.*

Gnocchetti Sardi al Ragù

SARDINIAN GNOCCHI WITH SAUCE

Gnocchi, Gnocchetti

A whole industry has developed around making short shaped pastas. Gnocchetti are round pasta shapes with a cavity, originally made with the thumb (see also Cavatelli, page 21). Depending on size, they are also called conchigliette or coccioline. The larger ones, about 12 mm (⅜ inch) in diameter are called tofarelle or mezze cocciolette. The exceptionally high-quality gnocchetti, also called malloreddus in Sardinia, come in three or four sizes, ranging from 5–30 mm (¼–1¼ inch) thick and are concave with a ribbed back. They are also made in the shape of huge shells by Sardinian women, who gather to make them for special occasions and celebrations.

4 tbsp olive oil

400 g (14 oz) knuckle or shoulder of pork, on the bone

1 onion, finely chopped

1 glass of dry white wine

a few bay leaves

a few juniper berries

700 g (1½ lb) polpa di pomodoro (tomato pulp)

1 tbsp tomato paste

500 g (1 lb 1½ oz) malloreddus (see Gnocchi, left)

60 g (2 oz) Sardinian hard pecorino cheese, grated

salt and pepper

Heat the oil in a large heavy-based pan, add the meat and brown on all sides. Add the onion and cook gently until soft, then stir in the wine, bay leaves and juniper berries. Simmer until the wine has evaporated, then add the tomato pulp and tomato paste, reduce the heat and cook gently for about 1½ hours. Season with salt and pepper to taste. Remove the meat from the pan and cut it into small strips, discarding the bone. Return the pieces of meat to the sauce.

Cook the pasta in lightly salted boiling water for 12–14 minutes or until *al dente*. Drain and mix with the sauce. Serve with pecorino cheese.

Window shopping at Pastificio Defilippis, Turin's celebrated specialist pasta shop.

Ragù alla Napoletana con Penne

PENNE WITH NEAPOLITAN RAGÙ

6 slices of beef topside, weighing about 125 g (4½ oz) each

1 garlic clove, thinly sliced

bunch of flat-leaf parsley, coarsely chopped

55 g (1¾ oz) pine nuts

55 g (1¾ oz) sultanas

60 g (2 oz) provola or parmesan cheese, grated

45 g (1½ oz) lard

25 g (¾ oz) Parma ham fat

2 glasses of red wine

2 tbsp tomato paste

450 g (1 lb) penne

salt and pepper

Season the beef. Mix together the garlic, parsley, pine nuts, sultanas and grated cheese, then divide this mixture between the slices of beef and roll them up. Secure with wooden cocktail sticks.

Heat the lard and fat in a heavy pan and brown the beef rolls all over. Add the wine and tomato paste with water to three-quarters cover the meat. Cook slowly for about 2 hours, checking occasionally and adding more water if required. When the meat is tender, adjust the seasoning.

Cook the pasta in boiling salted water until *al dente*, then drain. Serve the meat and sauce on the pasta.

Serves 6

In Naples, Sunday is not Sunday without *ragù*.

Provolone

This peculiar cheese originated in the Basilicata in the province of Potenza and from there it spread all over Italy.

It is a compact full-fat cheese made of cows' milk. After the rennet and relevant fermenting agents have been added, the curds are spun in hot water and worked into a large pear-shaped or cylindrical cheese, weighing at least 5.9 kg (13 lb). After they have been shaped, they are placed in giant containers and immersed in brine before being hung and bound by special strings which give them their distinctive shape.

*The maturing process takes about 12 months, depending on whether the cheese is to be eaten fresh (*tipo dolce*) or aged for grating (*piccante*). The matured cheese is covered with a thin layer of wax to prevent bacterial contamination. It is also known as provoloncino or provoletta, as well as many other names depending on the region.*

Provolone is eaten as a table cheese and used in cooking, in stuffings for vegetables and timbales, and also grated on pasta. It has a distinctive texture and flavour, the tipo piccante *sometimes tasting quite sharp.*

Timballo di Ziti

BAKED TIMBALE OF ZITI PASTA

Ziti

Today ziti is only made commercially, using durum wheat semolina and water. It is generally more popular in the South than the North, and over the years has somehow become the symbol of the South, and of Naples in particular. It is a long tubular pasta up to 5 cm (2 inches) in length and with a diameter of about 1 cm (½ inch) and a smooth surface. Cut into shorter tubes, it makes ditali, and cut into slightly longer tubes, maccheroni. If the sections are cut obliquely it makes penne.

If the ziti have a large diameter they are called mezze zite or boccolotti mezzani, while the largest are called zitoni or candele. If broken into irregularly shaped pieces they can be cooked and eaten either with a strong meat ragù or mixed with strong cheeses like caciocavallo, provola, pecorino or mozzarella, and sometimes sliced aubergines, to make pasticci.

1 kg (2¼ lb) long ziti
125 ml (4 fl oz) virgin olive oil
700 g (1½ lb) lean minced pork
250 g (9 oz) Neapolitan salami, cut into slices then into thin strips
2 large onions, finely chopped
1 glass of dry white wine
1.4 kg (3 lb) polpa di pomodoro (tomato pulp)
350 g (12 oz) hard caciocavallo or matured provolone cheese, grated
8 eggs, beaten
salt and pepper
freshly grated nutmeg

Cook the pasta in boiling salted water for 4 minutes, until pliable but not too soft, then drain and set aside.

Heat the olive oil in a large pan, add the pork and the salami and brown the meat, stirring from time to time to break up the lumps of minced pork. Add the onions and some nutmeg and cook until the onions are tender. Add the wine and boil until evaporated. Stir in the tomato pulp and cook gently for 2 hours. Add salt and pepper to taste and allow to cool a little.

Preheat the oven to 180°C/350°F/gas 4. Line a deep baking dish with some of the pasta. Mix the rest of the pasta with the sauce and stir in 300 g (10½ oz) of the grated cheese and the beaten eggs. Fill the baking dish with the mixture, sprinkle the remaining cheese on top and bake in the oven for 40 minutes. Carefully turn it out on to a serving dish and cut into slices to serve.

Serves 10

Tagliatelle al Ragù Bolognese

TAGLIATELLE WITH BOLOGNESE SAUCE

500 g (1 lb) fresh tagliatelle or 400 g (14 oz)
dried egg tagliatelle

60 g (2 oz) parmesan cheese, grated

FOR THE RAGÙ:

55 g (1¾ oz) butter

55 g (1¾ oz) minced prosciutto fat or pancetta

1 large carrot, finely chopped

1 celery stalk, finely chopped

1 onion, finely chopped

100 g (3½ oz) minced lean veal or beef

100 g (3½ oz) minced lean pork

1 glass of dry red wine

a little beef or chicken stock

3 tbsp tomato paste

salt and pepper

To make the *ragù*, heat the butter in a large pan, add the prosciutto fat
or pancetta, carrot, celery and onion and fry gently for 10 minutes. Add
the minced meats and stir with a wooden spoon to break them up. Cook
for about 15 minutes to brown the meat, then add the wine and bubble
for a few minutes. Stir in a little stock to prevent sticking. Stir in the
tomato paste and dilute with a few tablespoons of stock to give a sauce-
like consistency. Leave to simmer for 1½ hours, adding more stock if
the mixture becomes dry. At the end of the cooking time, add a little
more stock to obtain a smooth consistency. Season.

Cook the tagliatelle in boiling salted water until *al dente*, then drain
and mix with the sauce. Serve with the parmesan cheese.

Tagliatelle

*Tagliare means 'to cut', hence the name for
this Emilia-Romagnan pasta, which is cut
with a knife from a very thin sheet of egg
dough. Pasta ribbons can easily be made by
hand by simply cutting to any width from a
single sheet of pasta. To do this, simply
roll up a sheet of pasta and cut it to the
width desired then unroll each little disc of
pasta to reveal the long strands.*

*Tagliatelle and similar pasta ribbons,
like the thinner tagliolini and tagliarini,
can be dressed with ragùs of meat, tomato,
or seafood (for smaller varieties), as well
as pesto and mushroom sauces. Mixed
green and yellow tagliolini gives the effect
of 'straw and hay' in the traditional* paglia
e fieno, *mostly dressed with a creamy ham
and cheese sauce.*

Vincisgrassi

MEAT AND VEGETABLE LASAGNE

900 g (2 lb) fresh spinach

3 eggs

150 g (5 oz) parmesan cheese, grated

about 1 tbsp breadcrumbs

2 large aubergines, cut into slices 5 mm (¼ inch) thick

450 g (1 lb) large porcini, sliced

6 small, thin courgettes

1 recipe quantity of basic pasta dough (see page 9)

1 recipe quantity of Bolognese Ragù (see page 55)

400 g (14 oz) fontina cheese, thinly sliced

salt and pepper

freshly grated nutmeg

olive oil for frying

seasoned flour, for dusting

Wash the spinach, put it in a pan with just the water clinging to it and cook for a few minutes until wilted. Squeeze out all excess liquid. Chop roughly and mix with 1 egg, 30 g (1 oz) of the parmesan, and nutmeg and salt to taste. Stir in the breadcrumbs to give a binding consistency, then form the mixture into small balls. Heat olive oil for deep-frying and fry the balls until golden brown. Drain on paper towels.

Lightly beat together the 2 remaining eggs. Dust the aubergine slices with seasoned flour, dip them in the beaten egg and then shallow-fry them in a good layer of olive oil until golden. Drain and set aside. Shallow-fry the porcini in olive oil, too, then season.

Cook the whole courgettes in boiling salted water until just tender, then drain.

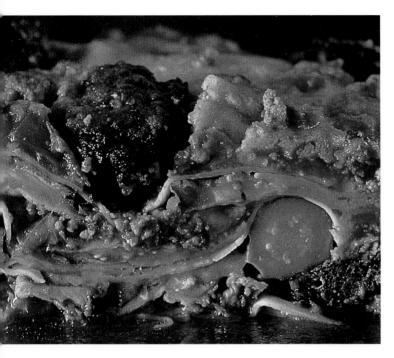

Lasagne

To help make the layers of lasagne and produce a lighter and more airy dish, some lasagnes are given a curled or corrugated edge; these are known as lasagna riccia, which are 35 mm (1½ inch) wide, and lasagnetta doppio riccio (half as wide) a smaller curly-edged lasagne.

The widest industrially made lasagne are called lasagnoni and are usually 8–10 cm (3¼–4 inches) wide and about 20 cm (8 inches) long. This is the only type of pasta that requires a little oil in the water when cooking to avoid the sheets sticking together. A smaller version of this curly pasta is called arricciata tripolini or signorine and are only 5 mm (¼ inch) wide, while mafalde or fettuccelle ricce is 12 mm (⅜ inch) wide and manfredi, trinette and mezza lasagna are all 20 mm (¾ inch) wide. All these pasta are eaten with tomato sauces and ragùs of beef, pork, lamb or game. They are also used to make pasticci.

Due to its versatility, lasagne has become one of the most popular dishes considered to be 'convenience food', not just in Italy but worldwide. It can be, and is mostly, prepared in large quantities industrially and then distributed in supermarkets either chilled or frozen.

Preheat the oven to 200°C/400°F/gas 6. Roll out the pasta dough and cut it into sheets of lasagne. Cook the lasagne in a large pan of boiling salted water for 3–4 minutes or until *al dente*. Drain on a tea towel.

Take a deep 20 x 30 cm (8 x 12 inch) baking tray and spread a third of the *ragù* over the bottom. Cover with a layer of lasagne, then a third of the fontina and parmesan, then half the fried aubergines and mushrooms. Add more sauce and another layer of lasagne, then arrange the whole courgettes on top lengthwise. Cover with another third of the cheese and the remaining aubergines and mushrooms. Finish with a layer of sauce, then the spinach balls and the remaining cheese. Bake in a hot oven for 30 minutes, until golden brown on top. Remove and leave to set for 10 minutes before cutting into squares to serve.
Serves 10

Glossary of Pasta Types

Agnolini / *Stuffed Pasta*
Agnolini is a small stuffed egg pasta, similar in shape to cappelletti, which can only be made by hand. Fillings are placed in the centre of circles of pasta, which are then folded over to make semi-circles. The corners of the semi-circle are bent round until they touch, to form little rings. Agnolini come from Lombardy and Emilia-Romagna.

Agnolotti / *Stuffed Pasta*
Great confusion is caused by the variety of names given to this pasta in different parts of Italy. Very like ravioli, these are little square cushions of stuffed egg pasta.

Alfabeto, Lettere /
Alphabet Pasta
This is simply a durum wheat semolina pasta extruded from a special die and cut very short into shapes like letters of the alphabet. Used in soups, they are often made with extra gluten for serving to children.

Anelli, Anellini / *Pasta Shape*
(Rings)
This is a ring-shaped durum wheat semolina pasta which is very popular in Sicily but quite difficult to obtain in other regions. It comes in various sizes, the smallest, anellini, being used in soups.

Anolini / *Stuffed Pasta*
This smallest type of tortellini is typical of the cuisine of Parma. Because they are so tiny, they are usually handmade, formed round a woman's little finger.

Bucatini / *Hollow Noodle*
Mostly used in Campania, Lazio and Liguria, this long pasta is slightly larger than spaghettoni but has a buco, or small hole, through the middle, making it easier to cook. Similar pastas include perciatellini and fidelini bucati. Larger versions include perciatelli and ziti.

Cannaroni Rigati / *Large Pasta Tubes*
This is one of the larger pasta shapes preferred in the South. Cannaroni or canneroni can be *lisci* (smooth) or *rigati* (fluted), but always have the same tubular shape and are usually at least 4 cm (1½ inches) long. They are popular in a number of regions and have many different names, from the larger *cannolicchi* and *denti di cavallo* (horse's tooth) to the smooth *sciviotti* and *occhio di lupo* (wolf's eye).

Cannelloni / *Large Stuffed Pasta Tubes*
This archetypal pasta from Emilia-Romagna is universally well-known, as its fame has been spread all over the world via Italian restaurants and trattorias. Today it is not only Italian manufacturers who make this large tubular pasta, it is made in many other countries as well.

Cannelloni was originally made with a sheet of rectangular pasta that was cooked as usual in boiling water, drained and rolled around a filling of meat, vegetables or even fish, then baked in a tomato sauce and topped with mozzarella or a béchamel sauce and parmesan. Now pasta manufacturers have developed ready-made tubes about 12.5 cm (5 inches) long, which are easier to fill.

Capelli d'Angelo / *Angel's Hair Pasta*
Resembling long strands of blond hair, hence the name capelli d'angelo (angel's hair), this long pasta is also known as fidelini or capellini and is the thinnest form of spaghetti you can find. It cooks very quickly so you will need to keep a close eye on the cooking time. There is also a black version, coloured with cuttlefish ink, which is mostly used with seafood sauces.

Cappelletti, Cappellettini / *Little Hat*
Resembling a hat (cappello), from which it gets its name, this handmade egg pasta is the trademark of Emilia-Romagna. There

is a smaller version called cappellettini. Cappelletti are similar to tortellini but differ mostly in that the filling is made of beef, pork and veal fried in butter, with some cubed Parma ham and parmesan.

Casônséi / *Stuffed Pasta*
Originating in Lombardy, this stuffed pasta is a speciality of the Valcamonica Valley. A rectangle of pasta is folded several times to make a dumpling shaped like a plaited loaf, which is then filled with potatoes, greens, mortadella, pork sausage, parmesan, eggs, garlic, breadcrumbs and parsley. The Veneto produces casonziei, a stuffed egg pasta similar to casônséi, but folded into a circular plait rather than a rectangular one. The filling is made of spinach, prosciutto, San Daniele ham, eggs, parmesan, and a little butter and cinnamon. There are many similar types of pasta with much the same basic filling but a slightly different shape.

Cavatelli, Cavatieddi, Cavatiddi, Cecatelli / *Pugliese Handmade Pasta*
This typical southern Italian speciality is made of durum wheat semolina and water. Cavatelli are made of pieces of dough about 2–3 cm (¾–1¼ inch) long which are pressed and pushed with the thumb to make a curved and slightly hollowed oval shape. The name comes from *cavare*, meaning 'to

dig', because of the movement needed to make the shape, although it is called strascinati in Basilicata.

Chifferi / *Pasta Shape (Elbows)*
This manufactured durum wheat semolina pasta is in the shape of a curved tube about 3–4 cm (1¼–1½ inches) in length and looks like an elbow. It probably gets its name from the Austrian bread or biscuit called a *kipferl*, which is curved into a croissant-like shape. There is a smaller version of this shape called mezzi gomiti (half elbows) as well as the similarly shaped gobboni (with a hump), stortoni (curved) and gozzettoni. All come both smooth (*lisci*) and fluted (*rigati*).

Chiocciole, Lumache, Lumachelle / *Pasta Shape (Snails)*
Mostly eaten in Campania and Liguria, these are types of pasta in the shape of a snail's shell and can be either smooth or fluted. They come in a range of sizes.

Chitarra, Manfricoli, Tonnarelli / *Square Spaghetti*
Called maccheroni alla chitarra in Abruzzo, manfricoli in Umbria and tonnarelli in Lazio, this long pasta is very much like spaghetti, except that it has a square section rather than round. It is made by laying a flat sheet of pasta over a special cutter made of many closely spaced steel wires called a *chitarra*. The sheet of pasta is pressed through

the wires with a rolling pin. The thickness of the pasta is equal to the distance between the wires so that when it goes through the *chitarra*, it is cut neatly into long square strands.

Cialzons / *Sweet Stuffed Pasta*
This sweet Friulian version of casonziei, made especially in Carnia, is the result of Austrian influences. The filling of spinach, raisins, candied peel, cinnamon and chocolate is contained in a semicircular pocket of pasta.

Conchiglie, Conchiglioni, Conchigliette / *Pasta Shells*
This shell-like pasta shape from Campania has a ribbed surface and thus collects lots of sauce. Because of its structure, however, it also takes about 15 minutes to cook. A larger version of the same shape, called conchiglioni, is often stuffed, usually with spinach and ricotta. Conchigliette is a small version used in soups and made with extra gluten for children. See Alfabeto.

Corzetti / *Ligurian Handmade Pasta*
This Ligurian speciality pasta, typical of the Polcevera Valley, uses a dough made with both egg and water (only 1 egg per 300 g of flour). A small round piece of dough is then pressed with both thumbs to produce a figure-of-eight shape about 2 x 5 cm (¾ x 2 inches) in size. There is also a

variety of corzetti called stampati, meaning 'pressed', made with a specially constructed wooden tool with a carved design etched into it that is transferred on to the pasta.

Culingiones / Sardinian Ravioli
This Sardinian contribution to stuffed pasta is rectangular in shape and filled with Swiss chard leaves, grated nutmeg, eggs and fresh and grated aged pecorino. In some areas the little pockets are pinched shut in artistic ways.

Ditali, Ditalini, Ditaloni, Tubetti / Pasta Shapes (Thimbles)
A dried pasta from Campania, ditali are closely associated with Neapolitan cooking. The name describes its shape, that of a little thimble, and these short pasta tubes come in a variety of sizes.

The smallest, called ditalini, are used in broths; the larger ditali are used in thicker vegetable soups, while the largest, ditaloni, are dressed with a variety of sauces.

Farfalle, Farfalline, Farfallette, Farfalloni / Pasta Shape (Butterflies, Little Bows)
Shaped like a butterfly, this pasta shape is usually commercially manufactured, although it can easily be made by hand using fresh pasta. To make it, cut long ribbons of pasta 3–4 cm (1¼–1½ inch) wide from a sheet of dough and then divide the ribbons into sections about 2–3 cm (¾–1¼ inch) long. Pinch each rectangle of pasta in the centre, pushing the edges together in the middle to make the butterfly shape. Farfalle are mainly eaten in Northern Italy.

A small version, variously called farfalline, canestrini and tripolini and of about 13 mm (⅝ inch) in length, is used in brodo while farfallette, called stricchetti in Bologna, are larger at 3 cm (1¼ inches) and are used in thicker soups.

Fusilli / Pasta Shape (Spirals)
Fusilli were first made in Campania by hand and were probably the first semolina pasta to have been made with a dough of just semolina and water, like Sicilian maccheroni. The technique has not changed much over the centuries and today it is still made by hand in Campania and Puglia and sold for a high price. The easiest way to buy fusilli nowadays is in dried form. Commercial imitations of fusilli have produced spiral shapes in many colours. Similar pastas to fusilli include elicoidale, spirale and eliche, a Southern version of fusilli with a substantial consistency that is now used all over Italy.

Garganelli / Handmade Pasta
This handmade egg pasta can be found only in Emilia-Romagna, where it was created. The egg pasta dough is made in the usual way, but with the addition of grated parmesan cheese and grated nutmeg. To make the garganelli a special gadget is needed which gives the outside a ribbed texture.

Gnocchi, Gnocchetti / Little Dumplings
It is very difficult to distinguish between gnocchetti and other similar pastas like cavatielli, conchiglie, chiocciole or lumache. All were created in response to the practice of boiling small, shapeless pieces of coloured semolina-and-water dough in water and then serving them with butter and parmesan.

With the entry of the potato into the culinary world, gnocchi started to be made with flour and potatoes instead of the standard semolina dough, and it is this which distinguishes them, making gnocchi di patate one of the first handmade pasta specialities.

Grandine / Pasta Shape
Grandine, literally meaning 'hailstone', is as its name suggests shaped like a very small round dot. It is made by cutting the thickest freshly make spaghetti into lengths of only a few millimetres. It is used in soups and broths only.

Lasagne, Lagane, Laganelle / Flat Pasta Sheets
In Naples this wide, flat sheet of semolina-and-water pasta is called laganelle, the name used by the Romans, although it is not known whether in ancient times the pasta was fried, baked or boiled. In

Campania lasagne are called lagane, in Calabria laganedde and in Basilicata, laane. Whatever the name used to describe it, lasagne are made from a long sheet of pasta rolled to a thickness of about 1 mm (¹⁄₂₄ inch) and cut in widths of about 3 cm (1¼ inches), although laganelle are just 1 cm (½ inch) wide.

Lasagnette / *Pasta Shape*
Also known as festoni, riccioline, reginette and lasagnette ricce, these are long, flat, wide pasta ribbons with curled edges, which prevent them sticking together during cooking and make them ideal for collecting more of the sauce. This type of pasta is not cut like tagliatelle but extruded through a die.

Maccheroni, Maccheroncelli / *Macaroni*
Historians cannot agree about where maccheroni originally came from. Some think maccheroni was first made in Sicily and is the result of the Arabic influence, while others attribute it to the Ligurians. Indeed, centuries ago Genova had the monopoly in the grain trade in the Mediterranean; hence its long tradition of pasta making.

Irrespective of its exact historical origins, maccheroni is synonymous with Italy. The term indicates a series of short pasta tubes, either smooth or fluted, like maccheroncelli, sedani rigati, maniche and many others. In the South, and especially in Naples, maccheroni is a generic term for all types of pasta. For example, the *frittata di maccheroni*, a pasta omelette so beloved of the Neapolitans, may use any type of pasta, including vermicelli, linguine and bucatini.

Maccherone includes pasta shapes such as cannolicchi medi, cannolicchi grandi, sciviottini, fagiolini, fischiotti, dente di pecora, dente di cavallo and many more.

Malfatti / *Dumplings*
Literally meaning 'badly made', the name for these little gnocchi refers to their irregular shapes. Apart from flour and eggs, they may contain chopped spinach or Swiss chard and either mascarpone or ricotta cheese.

Maltagliati / *Pasta Shape*
Literally meaning 'badly cut', maltagliati are made by cutting irregular shapes from a thinly rolled sheet of pasta. Mostly found in Emilia-Romagna, small pieces are used in pasta e fagioli and larger pieces are dressed with sauces.

Maniche, Gigantoni / *Pasta Shape (Large Tubes, Arms)*
This is a large, straight hollow pasta tube about 6 cm (2½ inches) in length and 1.5 cm (⅝ inch) in diameter. The outside can be smooth or ribbed, when they resemble rigatoni. In maniche, the tubes are slightly curved. They are especially popular in the South, where large shapes are preferred.

Marille / *Pasta Shape*
Marille was created by a car designer, Giorgetto Giugiaro, under commission from a pasta company in Campania. The idea was to design a pasta shape that would absorb and retain an abundant amount of sauce, so that each piece of pasta would become a juicy morsel in its own right. The pasta was designed on a drawing board and is made of two tubes joined together. It is ribbed on the inside and smooth on the outside, with an aerodynamic wing attached to the side of one of the tubes. It holds the sauce inside.

Marubini / *Stuffed Pasta*
This is a large, round ravioli-type pasta with a serrated edge. It is a speciality of Cremona and comes with two types of filling. The first consists of walnuts, parmesan, eggs, breadcrumbs and nutmeg.

Pasticcio, Pasticciata, Pasta 'ncasciata / *Pasta Pie*
The origins of the *pasticcio* probably lie with medieval Tuscan chefs mimicking the pies of Elizabethan England; and in those days the *pasticcio* would probably have contained meat.

Nowadays, however, most consist of a pastry shell containing a filling of cooked pasta, like tortellini, layered with cheeses and tomato sauce. Every region now has its own variation, like the pasta 'ncasciata of Sicily.

Pizzoccheri / *Buckwheat Noodle*
Pizzoccheri is a long pasta typical of a valley in Lombardy called Valtellina, where the pasta dough is traditionally made with a mixture of one-third 00 (*doppio zero*) flour and two-thirds buckwheat flour.

Rigatoni / *Fluted Pasta Shape (Tubes)*
Rigatoni is a group of large pasta tube shapes that are ribbed on the outside and served with meat *ragù* or other strong sauces, or baked in the oven. All of the various pasta shapes included in this group are quite large, being about 5-6 cm (2-2½ inches) in length and 1-2 cm (¼ - ¾ inches) in diameter.

Ruote, Rotelline / *Pasta Shape (Wheels)*
Made in the shape of a wheel, this is an example of a pasta which has no special use except being pretty.

Sedani / *Pasta Shape (Tubes)*
Literally translated sedani means 'celery' because the shape of this pasta resembles a small stick of celery. Probably from the same group as maccheroni, it is mainly used in Southern Italy and is a hollow pasta which can have either a smooth or ribbed surface.

Spaghetti, Spaghettini, Vermicelli, Vermicellini
The area around Naples has the type of air, climate and water which makes it natural to produce vermicelli, meaning 'little worms' (the term favoured for spaghetti in the South), which can still be found drying in the sun there.

The dough for Neapolitan pasta is a mixture of hard durum semolina flour and water. The cooking time varies from 4–5 minutes for fine pasta and 8–9 minutes for the larger.

Strangolapreti, Strangulaprievete, Strozzapreti / *Long Pasta, Dumplings*
Priests in Italy are assumed to possess even more than the normal healthy Italian appetite, hence these names (all meaning 'priest strangler') for various types of pasta, related specialities and dishes in the different regions.

In Puglia, the term is used for a type of twisted pasta; in Abruzzi *strozzapreti* for extra-long spaghetti; in Naples and Campania *strangulaprievete* is applied to potato gnocchi; and in the North it is used mostly to describe a type of dumpling.

Tagliatelle, Tagliolini, Tagliarini, Fettucce, Fettuccine, Piccagge, Pappardelle / *Flat Pasta Ribbons*
These long flat pasta ribbons come in a variety of widths and so go under a number of names depending on the region, but are basically tagliatelle or fettuccine. Fettuccine is associated mainly with central Italy around Rome, while its close relative, tagliatelle (a little wider and thinner) is northern, with Bologna its main centre. Generally, the further south you go, the thicker the pasta ribbons.

Tajarin / *Pasta Ribbon*
This Piedmontese pasta is a local version of tagliolini, which is 2.5 mm (⅛ inch) wide and probably the smallest type of fresh cut pasta.

Tortelli, Tortellini, Tortelloni, Tordello, Cappellacci / *Stuffed Pasta*
Depending on the region, tortelli may be square or round, and filled with all sorts of ingredients.

Trenette / *Long Pasta*
Trenette is a flat and long Ligurian pasta, similar to bavette but slightly larger. It is eaten exclusively with Genovese pesto sauce.

Tubetti, Tubettini / *Pasta Shape (Tubes)*
These small pasta tubes are used in soups such as minestrone and for *pasta e fagioli*.

Zite, Ziti, Zitoni / *Pasta Shape (Tubes)*
Today ziti are only made commercially, using durum wheat semolina. Ziti is generally more popular in the South, and over the years has somehow become the symbol of the south, and of Naples in particular. It is a smooth tubular pasta up to 5 cm (2 inches) in length and with a diameter of about 1 cm (½ inch).

Index

Publishing Director: Anne Furniss
Creative Director: Mary Evans
Editor: Lewis Esson
Consultant Art Director: Helen Lewis
Design: Sue Storey
Cover Design: Claire Peters
Assistant Editor: Jane Middleton
Editorial Assistant: Rhian Bromage
Production: Sarah Neesam &
                Vincent Smith

This edition first published in 2013 by
Quadrille Publishing Limited,
Alhambra House,
27-31 Charing Cross Road,
London WC2H OLS

Based on material originally published
in *Carluccio's Complete Italian Food.*

Text © 1997 & 1999 Carluccio's
Partnership
Photography © 1997 Estate of
Andre Martin
Cover Illustrations © 2013
Zack Blanton
Design, edited text and layout © 1999,
2013 Quadrille Publishing Ltd

The rights of the authors have been
asserted.

Cataloguing-in-Publication Data: a
catalogue record for this book is
available from the British Library.

ISBN 978 184949 480 9

Printed in China.